The Donner Party: The Tragic Story of the  Most Notorious Journey

By Charles River Editors

Drawing of the Truckee Lake camp based on descriptions by William Graves, survivor of the Donner Party

About Charles River Editors

Charles River Editors provides superior editing and original writing services across the digital publishing industry, with the expertise to create digital content for publishers across a vast range of subject matter. In addition to providing original digital content for third party publishers, we also republish civilization's greatest literary works, bringing them to new generations of readers via ebooks.

Sign up here to receive updates about free books as we publish them, and visit Our Kindle Author Page to browse today's free promotions and our most recently published Kindle titles.

Introduction

Map of the route of the Donner Party made by K. Musser

The Donner Party

"Like fated trains of other epochs whose privations, sufferings, and self-sacrifices have added renown to colonization movements and served as danger signals to later wayfarers, that party began its journey with song of hope, and within the first milestone of the promised land ended it with a prayer for help. 'Help for the helpless in the storms of the Sierra Nevada Mountains!'" – Eliza P. Donner Houghton, *The Expedition of the Donner Party and Its Tragic Fate*

The westward movement of Americans in the 19th century was one of the largest and most consequential migrations in history, and for countless people back east, the West represented opportunities for adventure, independence, and fortune. Even in the 21st century, Americans look back on the era fondly, even romantically, and millions are familiar with the popular game that reignited interest in the Oregon Trail

Of course, it's easy for people with modern transportation to comfortably reminisce about the West, because many pioneers discovered that the traveling was fraught with various kinds of obstacles and danger, including bitter weather, potentially deadly illnesses, and hostile Native Americans, not to mention an unforgiving landscape that famous American explorer Stephen Long deemed "unfit for human habitation." 19th century Americans were all too happy and eager for the transcontinental railroad to help speed their passage west and render overland paths obsolete.

One of the main reasons people yearned for new forms of transportation is because of the most notorious and tragic disasters in the history of westward travel. While people still romanticize the Wild West, many Americans are still all too familiar with the fate of the Donner Party, a group of 87-90 people that met with disaster in the Sierra Nevada mountain range during the winter of

1846-1847. The party knew the journey would take months, but early snowfalls in the mountains left dozens of people trapped in snow drifts that measured several feet, stranding them in a manner that made it virtually impossible for them to go any further for several weeks.

Inevitably, as the Donner Party's supplies began to run low, there was little hope of acquiring new provisions high up in the mountains, and even worse, their location and the technology of the time also made it virtually impossible for relief expeditions to reach them. Due to exposure and lack of food, the health of many in the party began to deteriorate quickly in the tough winter conditions, and the animals brought along with the group died at alarming rates. Most of the men who set out to try to get help died en route, while the families back in camp tried to cope with dozens of deaths suffered by young and old alike.

As a few able-bodied men went for help, the people who remained back in their wagons resorted to the most desperate of measures in attempts to either stay alive or keep their children alive. Some members of the Donner Party fought with each other, occasionally fatally, and the journey is perhaps best known today for accounts of cannibalism. One member of the group noted in his diary in February 1847, "Mrs Murphy said here yesterday that thought she would Commence on Milt. & eat him. I dont that she has done so yet, it is distressing."

All the while, the plight of the Donner Party made news across the nation, even before the surviving members were rescued and brought to safety, and by the time the doomed expedition was over, less than 50 of them made it to California. As writer Ethan Rarick summed it up, "more than the gleaming heroism or sullied villainy, the Donner Party is a story of hard decisions that were neither heroic nor villainous."

The Donner Party: The Tragic Story of the Wild West's Most Notorious Journey chronicles one of the most ill-fated journeys in American history Along with pictures of important people, places, and events, you will learn about the Donner Party like never before, in no time at all.

The Donner Party: The Tragic Story of the Wild West's Most Notorious Journey
About Charles River Editors
Introduction
   Chapter 1: Preparing for a Trip West
   Chapter 2: Joining the Wagon Train
   Chapter 3: The First Big Mistake
   Chapter 4: Another Mistake
   Chapter 5: Death and Snow
   Chapter 6: The Forlorn Hope
   Chapter 7: "The Terrible Necessity"
   Chapter 8: Survival
   Chapter 9: Rescue
   Chapter 10: Life From Death
Bibliography

Chapter 1: Preparing for a Trip West

"It is supposed there be 7000 wagons start from this place, this season. We go to California, to the bay of Francisco. It is a four months trip. We have three wagons furnished with food & clothing, etc. drawn by three yoke of oxen each. We take cows along & milk them & have some butter though not as much as we would like. I am willing to go & have no doubt it will be an advantage to our children & to us." - Tamsen Donner

The modern world is often surprised by what the Donner Party began as and always shocked by how it ended, but while the outcome was understandably shocking, the beginning of the journey was anything but. It's safe to say that had almost everyone survived the journey they planned months earlier, their names would be lost among the records of the thousands of settlers that made their way west during the 1840s and 1850s. Some became famous for their successes; but the Donner Party is infamous for its failure.

Of course, no one set out to fail, least of all the two extended families that gathered together in April 1846 to begin their journey. The Donner's, whose family lent their name to the tragedy, were led by George, his brother Jacob, and their respective wives, Tamsen and Elizabeth. Between them, they had 12 young children, including George's daughters Elitha (14), Leanna (12), Frances (6), Georgia (4) and Eliza (3), and Jacob's children, Solomon (14), William Hook (a 12 year old whom Elizabeth brought from her first marriage), George (9), Mary (7), Isaac (4), Lewis (4) and Samuel (1).

The second family was led by James Reed and his wife, Margaret, who had four children: Virginia (13), Patty (8), James (5) and Thomas (3). They were also accompanied by Margaret's mother, Sarah Keyes, who was 70 years old and already dying of tuberculosis, which was known in the 19th century as consumption. In addition to the families, there were 10 hired men: Hiram O. Miller, Samuel Shoemaker, Noah James, Charles Burger, John Denton, Augustus Spitzer, Milt Elliot, James Smith, Walter Herron, and Baylis Williams. Their primary duties were to drive and care for the livestock accompanying the party, while Baylis Williams' 25 year old sister, Eliza, went with them to help with the cooking.

James and Margaret Reed

Patty Reed

    The little group set out from Springfield, Illinois in nine wagons on April 14, 1946, and they were among 500 wagons that began a similar trek west that year. Their timing was important, because it was imperative that they cross the prairies during the summer months when the ripe grass would keep their livestock fed, and they also had to cross the mountains far enough into fall that the mud had dried but early enough that the snow had not yet begun. The men knew, and had probably told their wives, that timing was the most important factor in their survival, and if the Donner Party was unaware of that at the beginning of their journey, they certainly learned it by the end.

The first few weeks of the trip were uneventful, and most were still plenty optimistic about the future. The children ran barefooted beside the wagons, wiggling their toes appreciatively in the soft grass, and the provisions were still fresh and only had to last for a little while because the group could restock at least once more on the trip. On May 10, they arrived in Independence, where they stocked up with more supplies for the trip and were joined by Charles Stanton, a young man whom the Donner's invited to join their group. He dashed off a quick letter to his brother and posted it just before they left. It read, in part, "Well what may surprise you perhaps is that I am going to start for California tomorrow. I met with a good opportunity and, thinking it doubtful whether I should find anything to do in this country I concluded to go...If you have never read Hastings Oregon & California get it and read it. You will see some of the inducements which led me to this step. I am in hopes to get through safe which I think there is little danger as we go in such large crowds that we shall be law unto ourselves and a protection unto each other"

Charles Stanton

Eliza Donner was about 4 years old that summer, and she later described her memories about the group's stop in Independence, Missouri:

> "We reached Independence, Missouri, on the eleventh of May, with our wagons and cattle in prime condition, and our people in the best of spirits. Our party encamped near that bustling frontier town, and were soon a part of the busy crowds, making ready for the great prairie on the morrow. Teams thronged the highways; troops of men, women, and children hurried nervously about seeking information and replenishing supplies. Jobbers on the street were crying their wares, anxious to sell anything or everything required, from a shoestring to a complete outfit for a

four months' journey across the plains. Beads of sweat clung to the merchants' faces as they rushed to and fro, filling orders. Brawny blacksmiths, with breasts bared and sleeves rolled high, hammered and twisted red hot metal into the divers forms necessary to repair yokes and wagons…

"As we drove up Main Street, delayed emigrants waved us a light-hearted good-bye, and as we approached the building of the American Tract Society, its agent came to our wagons and put into the hand of each child a New Testament, and gave to each adult a Bible, and also tracts to distribute among the heathen in the benighted land to which we were going. Near the outskirts of town we parted from William Donner, took a last look at Independence, turned our backs to the morning sun, and became pioneers indeed to the Far West."

The group traveled along on their own for a few days before crossing over the Missouri state line, which metaphorically represented the beginning of the Western frontier to many in the party. According to one man who described the scene years later: ""In due time we arrived at a camp called the Lone Elm, across the Missouri line. This place was thought to be the limit of civilization, at this camp we met some hunters returning with furs & they gave us some dried buffalo meat and told us that we had no idea of what we would suffer before we reached California. This prediction proved too true – At this camp was an Elm tree the only tree of any kind in sight. I shall never forget the loneliness of the scene boy though I was at time. What made the matter still more lonelier we were only one family not having yet been joined by any other parties crossing the plains that year. Still we were fairly on our way across the plains, and were afterwards joined by other parties."

Chapter 2: Joining the Wagon Train

"I See no wagons bound for California that [are] as good as my family wagon and I have the opinion of all that has seen it here to that effect although there is fine wagon on the road where I [am] going to start again I would not change much in the plan...My dear Bro James I never in all my life Saw a more beautiful county, than that which we have passed through Since we left Missouri. It is as rich as the best land in Sangamon and so beautifully situated that a man could make a farm to suit in all directions but timber is scarce. [There are] springs in all directions although we came in a dividing ridge nearly all the time." - James Reed

On May 19, the Donner Party joined a wagon train of 50 wagon guided by William Russell, and among those traveling in this party was journalist Edwin Bryant. He wrote in his journal on May 20, "We were joined to-day by nine wagons from Illinois, belonging to Mr. Reed and the Messrs. Donner, highly respectable and intelligent gentlemen, with interesting families. They were received into the company by a unanimous vote." These sentiments were echoed by young Eliza Donner, who noted of that day:

"A new census of our party was taken this morning; and it was found to consist of 98 fighting men, 50 women, 46 wagons, and 350 cattle. Two divisions were made for convenience in travelling. We were joined to-day by nine wagons from Illinois belonging to Mr. Reed and Messrs. Donner, highly respectable and intelligent gentlemen with interesting families. They were received into the company by a unanimous vote. Our cattle were allowed to rest that day; and while the men were hunting and fishing, the women spread the family washings on the boughs and bushes of that well-wooded stream. We children, who had been confined to the wagon so many hours each day, stretched our limbs, and scampered off on Mayday frolics. We waded the creek, made mud pies, and gathered posies in the narrow glades between the cottonwood, beech, and alder trees. Colonel Russell was courteous to all; visited the new members, and secured their cheerful indorsement of his carefully prepared plan of travel. He was at the head of a representative body of pioneers, including lawyers, journalists, teachers, students, farmers, and day-laborers, also a minister of the gospel, a carriage-maker, a cabinet-maker, a stonemason, a jeweller, a blacksmith, and women versed in all branches of woman's work.

The government of these emigrant trains was essentially democratic and characteristically American. A captain was chosen, and all plans of action and rules and regulations were proposed at a general assembly, and accepted or rejected by majority vote. Consequently, Colonel Russell's function was to preside over meetings, lead the train, locate camping ground, select crossings over fordable streams, and direct the construction of rafts and other expedients for transportation over deep waters."

It was not long before the group had more company in the form of Native Americans. Young Virginia Reed, who had heard stories from her grandmother about "savages," was surprised by their demeanor and wrote decades later, "Nothing of much interest happened until we reached what is now Kansas. The first Indians we met were the Caws, who kept the ferry, and had to take us over the Caw River. I watched them closely, hardly daring to draw my breath, and feeing sure they would sink the boat in the middle of the stream, and was very thankful when I found they were not like Grandma's Indians."

By this time, James Reed was concerned about his mother-in-law's ability to stand the trip, given that her tuberculosis was liable to kill her at any time no matter where she was. James Reed wrote to her son, James Keyes, "I am afraid your mother will not stand it many weeks or indeed days, if there is not a quick change…I have been talking this moment with Your Mother. She says she feels very much like she was going to die. One of her eyes pains her much and she is so blind that she cannot take her coffee or plate if it is set near her this morning. She cannot eat anything. I am of opinion a few days will end her mortal career."

Though many thought that the group was off to a good start, there were some who were already concerned about the slow progress they were making. On May 24, journalist Edward Bryant wrote in his journal, "I am beginning to feel alarmed at the tardiness of our movements, and fearful that winter will find us in the snowy mountains of California, or that we shall suffer from the exhaustion of our supply of provisions. I do not fear for myself, but for the women and children of the emigrants. Singular as it may seem, there are many of our present party who have no just conceptions of the extent and labor of the journey before them."

A few days later, the group met another problem when they came to the Blue River, which was still swollen by the spring rains and snowmelt and thus could not be crossed for several days. They also had to deal with the death of Sarah Keyes, as James Reed had worriedly predicted. In a letter to her cousin, 12 year old Virginia Reed wrote, "We came to the Blue--the water was so high we had to stay there 4 days--in the meantime Gramma died. She became speechless the day before she died. We buried her very decent. We made a neat coffin and buried her under a tree we had a head stone and had her name cut on it and the date and year. Very nice, and at the head of the grave was a tree. We cut some letters on it. The young men sodded it all over and put flowers on it. We miss her very much every time we come into the Wagon. We look at the bed for her." With that, Sarah Keyes became the first member of the Donner Party to die, but unlike the others, her grave would remain undisturbed and would be commented on in the letters and journals of many who traveled the same path later. In fact, it's likely that few were aware of her connection to the doomed party.

While the Reed family prepared a decent burial for Keyes, the rest of the party was busy building rafts to try to get the wagons across the river. While such a crossing was obviously dangerous, it soon became clear that it was not as dangerous as waiting any longer, so the group finally made it across the "Big Blue" on May 31. Eliza Donner described the crossing: "The craft being finished on the morning of the thirtieth of May, was christened Blue Rover, and launched amid cheers of the company. Though not a thing of beauty, she was destined to fulfil the expectations of our worthy Captain. One set of guide-ropes held her in place at the point of embarkation, while swimmers on horseback carried another set of ropes across the river and quickly made them fast. Only one wagon at a time could cross, and great difficulty was experienced in getting the vehicles on and off the boat. Those working near the bank stood in water up to their arm-pits, and frequently were in grave peril. By the time the ninth wagon was safely landed, darkness fell. The only unforeseen delay that had occurred was occasioned by an awkward slip of the third wagon while being landed. The Blue Rover groaned under the shock, leaned to one side and swamped one of the canoes. However, the damage was slight and easily repaired. The next day was Sunday; but the work had to go on, and the Rev. Mr. Cornwall was as ready for it as the rest of the toilers."

During the period of time that the wagon train was at a standstill, a bit of controversy broke out over its leadership, and as a result, William Russell resigned as its captain and was replaced by

William Boggs. Boggs in turn would soon be replaced by another leader, and this frequent change in leadership was not a good omen for the future.

On June 12, the party reached another milestone when it crossed the famous Platte River. Tamsen Donner wrote to a friend, "We are now on the Platte, 200 miles from Fort Laramie. .... Wood is now very scarce, but 'Buffalo chips' are excellent--they kindle quick and retain heat surprisingly. We had this evening Buffalo steaks broiled upon them that had the same flavor they would have had upon hickory coals. We feel no fear of Indians. Our cattle graze quietly around our encampment unmolested. Two or three men will go hunting twenty miles from camp;--and last night two of our men lay out in the wilderness rather than ride their horses after a hard chase. Indeed if I do not experience something far worse than I have yet done, I shall say the trouble is all in getting started... George Donner is himself yet. He crows in the morning, and shouts out 'Chain up, boys!--chain up!' with as much authority as though he was 'something in particular.'"

As it turned out, George Donner's enthusiasm would ultimately prove to be their undoing.

Chapter 3: The First Big Mistake

"Col. Russell and his party, by hard traveling, reached Fort Bridger two or three days before the others...At that place they were met by Mr. Hastings, from California, who came out to conduct them in by the new route, by the foot of Salt Lake, discovered by capt. Fremont, which is said to be two hundred miles nearer than the old one, by Fort Hall. The distance to California was said to be six hundred and fifty miles, through a fine farming country, with plenty of grass for the cattle. Companies of from one to a dozen wagons ... are continually arriving, and several have already started on, with Hastings at their head, who would conduct them to near where the road joins the old route..." – *The Missouri Republican*

As the group made its way west, an important source of debate was over which route to take as they neared the modern states of Utah and Nevada. Eliza Donner explained why the leaders of the group were arguing with each other: "They were led to do so by 'An Open Letter,' which had been delivered to our company…by special messenger on horseback. The letter was written by Lansford W. Hastings, author of 'Travel Among the Rocky Mountains, Through Oregon and California.' It was dated and addressed, 'At the Headwaters of the Sweetwater: To all California Emigrants now on the Road,' and intimated that, on account of war between Mexico and the United States, the Government of California would probably oppose the entrance of American emigrants to its territory; and urged those on the way to California to concentrate their numbers and strength, and to take the new and better route which he had explored from Fort Bridger, by way of the south end of Salt Lake. It emphasized the statement that this new route was nearly two hundred miles shorter than the old one by way of Fort Hall and the headwaters of Ogden's River, and that he himself would remain at Fort Bridger to give further information, and to conduct the emigrants through to the settlement."

However, while camping at Fort Laramie in June, the party began to hear warnings about using

"Hastings Cutoff," the route they had planned to take over the mountains. It had been promoted to them by Hastings, who promised to meet them at Fort Bridger and lead them through to the other side of the Sierra Nevada Mountains. However, James Clyman, an old friend of Reed's, warned them about it and later explained, "Mr. Reed, while we were encamped at Laramie, was enquiring about the route. I told him to 'take the regular wagon track and never leave it--it is barely possible to get through it if you follow it--and it may be impossible if you don't.' Reed replied, 'There is a nigher route, and it is of no use to take so much of a roundabout course.' I admitted the fact, but told him about the great desert and the roughness of the Sierras, and that a straight route might turn out to be impracticable.'"

Clyman's warning was prescient, because as it turned out, Hastings was urging people to take the "Hastings Cutoff" despite having little familiarity with the terrain itself. Hastings claimed in *The Emigrant's Guide to Oregon and California*, "The most direct path would be leave the Oregon route, about two hundred miles east of Fort Hall; thence bearing west-south west, to the Salt Lake; and thence continuing down to the bay of San Francisco." In fact, not only did Hastings' path have all kinds of troublesome terrain, it actually added over 100 miles to the journey across the traditional California Trail, making it the worst kind of "shortcut".

Lansford Hastings

The trail to California in green with the Hastings Cutoff in red

The large party continued to discuss whether or not they should take the Hastings Cutoff or the traditional route, and the discussions continued though much of June as they continued west. On the 4th of July, the group enjoyed a hearty Independence Day, as described by Eliza Donner: "A salute was fired at sunrise, and later a platform of boxes was arranged in a grove close by, and by half-past nine o'clock every one in camp was in holiday attire, and ready to join the procession which marched around the camp and to the adjacent grove. There, patriotic songs were sung, the Declaration of Independence was read, and Colonel Russell delivered an address. After enjoying a feast prepared by the women of the company, and drinking to the health and happiness of friends and kindred in reverent silence, with faces toward the east, our guests bade us a final good-bye and godspeed."

After their July 4th celebration, William Russell led a group ahead of the others because he was determined to make it through before the snowfall. The rest of the company proceeded at a slower rate until July 18, when they split up; the Donner's and Reed's decided to continue on toward Fort Bridger, with George Donner now their elected leader. The other group continued along the longer route.

There were problems from the very start and warnings that the party might not be in the hands of the wisest leaders. Charles Stanton confided in his diary on the 18th, "In the morning, Saturday, we got an early start, and drove about ten or twenty miles and 'nooned,' without finding water for our cattle…After our usual delay, we were again on the road, and after a few hours' drive, came to a fine spring, with the grass looking green about it. The managers of our company finding it rather boggy…and concluded to go on till they found better grass…We presently came to a deep gully, where there was a little water, but no grass and were going by without paying it a passing notice, when Mr. R[eed], who had been sent on a head to look out for a camping place, was seen returning at full gallop…and told us that we must go back to the gully and stay, as bad as it was. It was after dark that night before we got our suppers. Mr. D[onner], who had been out with R. had not returned, and we all concluded that he must be lost. Guns were fired and beacons placed on the surrounding hills. At 12 o'clock, he made his appearance."

As the Donner Party continued west through late July, other members became dispirited. Eliza Donner noted that by July 20, her mother "was gloomy, sad, and dispirited in view of the fact that her husband and others could think of leaving the old road, and confide in the statement of a man of whom they knew nothing, but was probably some selfish adventurer." Indeed, the first blow that placed the Donner Party on the path to tragedy came on July 28 when they arrived at Fort Bridger and learned that Hastings had left without them, accompanied by those who had earlier broken away from their group. However, others at the fort encouraged the party to continue their journey, assuring them that the Hastings Cutoff was perfectly safe, and Hastings himself had left instructions claiming that there was "an abundant supply of wood, water, and pasturage along the whole line of road, except one dry drive of thirty miles, or forty at most; that they would have no difficult [canyons] to pass; and that the road was generally smooth, level, and hard."

Thus, on July 31, the Donner Party left Fort Bridger, guided only by information shared with them by a man now miles ahead of them on the treacherous trail. In addition to those already mentioned, the party also now included the Levinah Murphy family, made up of Levinah, her five youngest children, her two married daughters, her two sons-in-law, and her three grandchildren. Then there was William Eddy and his family, as well as Patrick and Peggy Breen and their seven children. Louis Keseberg was traveling with his wife Elizabeth and their two young children, the youngest of whom was actually born during the trip. The oldest person in the party was Mr. Hardkoop, then 60. Mr. and Mrs. Wolfinger had no children, but they were traveling with Mr. Wolfinger's business partner, Joseph Reinhardt. The group also picked up a few more families along the way, bringing their total number to 87 people travelling in 23 wagons.

Patrick Breen

William Eddy

William Murphy

In a July 31 letter to his brothers-in-law, James Reed was still brimming with enthusiasm over the plan: "I have replenished my stock by purchasing from Messrs. Vasques & Bridger, two very excellent and accommodating gentlemen, who are the proprietors of this trading post.--The new road, or Hastings' Cut-off, leaves the Fort Hall road here, and is said to be a saving of 350 or 400 miles in going to California, and a better route. There is, however, or thought to be, one stretch of 40 miles without water…The rest of the Californians went the long route--feeling afraid of Hasting's Cut-off. Mr. Bridger informs me that the route we design to take, is a fine level road, with plenty of water and grass, with the exception before stated." It wouldn't take long for Reed to discover that he and the rest of the party had been tragically misled.

Chapter 4: Another Mistake

"Bear River, August 3, 1846... I may not have another opportunity of sending you letters till I reach California...We take a new route to California, never traveled before this season;

consequently our route is over a new an interesting region. We are now in the Bear River valley, in the midst of the Bear River Mountains, the summits of which are covered with snow. As I am now writing, we are cheered by a warm summer's sun, while but a few miles off, the snow covered mountains are glittering in its beams." - Charles Stanton

On August 6, the Party reached the bank of the Weber River but found a letter from Hastings himself warning them not to continue. Reed would later explain, "Leaving Fort Bridger, we unfortunately took the new route, traveling on without incident of note, until we arrived at the head of Webber canyon. A short distance before reaching this place we found a letter sticking in the top of a sage bush. It was from Hastings. He stated that if we would send a messenger after him he would return and pilot us through a route much shorter and better than the canyon. A meeting of the company was held, when it was resolved to send Messrs. McCutchen, Stanton and myself to Mr. Hastings; also we were at the same time to examine the [canyon] and report at short notice."

Reed, Stanton, and McCutchen caught up with Hastings near the Great Salt Lake and persuaded him to return with them to point them to a better route. Leaving Stanton and McCutchen with his party, Hastings rode part of the way back with Reed and showed him a route that would lead through the Wasatch Mountains, but then he returned to his party and continued on his way. According to Reed, "After he gave me the direction, Mr. Hastings and I separated...After descending to what may be called the table land, I took an Indian trail and blazed the route where it was necessary that the road should be made, if the company so directed when they heard the report. When McCutchen, Stanton and myself got through Weber canyon on our way to overtake Mr. Hastings, our conclusions were that many of the wagons would be destroyed in attempting to get through the canyon ...I reached the company in the evening and reported to them the conclusions in regard to Weber canyon, at the same time stating that the route that I had blazed that day was fair, but would take considerable labor in clearing and digging. They agreed with unanimous voice to take that route if I would direct them in the road making, they working faithfully until it was completed."

Thus, the settlers began to clear away the brush, working slowly to create a path for the wagons to pass through, but they faced their biggest challenge to date on August 22. According to John Breen, "We at last came within one mile of Salt Lake Valley, when we were compelled to pass over a hill so steep that from ten to twelve yoke of oxen were necessary to draw each wagon to the summit. From this height we beheld the Great Salt Lake, and the extensive plains by which it is surrounded. It gave us great courage; for we thought we were going to have good roads through a fertile country." Eliza Donner also described the same scene: "We retraced our way, and after five days of alternate travelling and road-making, ascended a mountain so steep that six and eight yoke of oxen were required to draw each vehicle up the grade, and most careful handling of the teams was necessary to keep the wagons from toppling over as the straining cattle zigzaged to the summit. Fortunately, the slope on the opposite side was gradual and the last wagon descended to camp before darkness obscured the way. The following morning, we crossed the river which flows from Utah Lake to Great Salt Lake and found the trail of the Hastings party. We had been thirty days in reaching that point, which we had hoped to make in ten or twelve."

The party spent most of August 28 cutting grass to feed their cattle during their week-long trek across the desert, but then a misunderstanding brought new problems. James Reed later wrote, "We started to cross the desert traveling day and night only stopping to feed and water our teams as long as water and grass lasted. We must have made at least two-thirds of the way across when a great portion of the cattle showed signs of giving out. Here the company requested me to ride on and find the water and report. Before leaving I requested my principal teamster, that when my cattle became so exhausted that they could not proceed further with the wagons, to turn them out and drive them on the road after me until they reached the water, but the teamster misunderstanding unyoked them when they first showed symptoms of giving out, starting on with them for the water. I found the water about twenty miles from where I left the company and started on my return. About eleven o'clock at night, I met my teamsters with all my cattle and horses. I cautioned them particularly to keep the cattle on the road, for that as soon as they would scent the water they would break for it. I proceeded on and reached my family and wagons. Some time after leaving the man one of the horses gave out and while they were striving to get it along, the cattle scented the water and started for it. And when they started with the horses, the cattle were out of sight, they could not find them, or their trail, as they told me afterward." Though they later tried to round the cattle up, many were lost.

The party spent the first week in September camped along the base of Pilot Peak while recovering and repairing the damaged wagons, and with most of his cattle gone, Reed, Donner and Keseberg now decided to leave behind four of their wagons. The loss of the cattle meant the loss of milk and butter, and other foodstuffs were running low too, so Charles Stanton went ahead to Sutter's Fort with William McCutchen to get more supplies.

Chapter 5: Death and Snow

"Day after day, from dawn to twilight, we moved onward, never stopping, except to give the oxen the necessary nooning, or to give them drink when water was available. Gradually, the distance between sections lengthened, and so it happened that the wagons of my father and my uncle were two days in advance of the others, on the eighth of October, when Mr. Reed, on horseback, overtook us. He was haggard and in great tribulation. His lips quivered as he gave substantially the following account of circumstances which had made him…a lone wanderer in the wilderness." – Eliza Donner

After McCutchen returned, the party continued on its way, eventually rounding the Ruby Mountains and reaching the California Trail on September 26. By this time, however, emotions were running high, as the nights were beginning to get colder and the group was not even near the mountains yet. On October 5, a dispute broke out between Reed and John Snyder, one of the men who had joined the group later. According to Eliza Furhman, "The men were irritable and impatient. A dispute arose one day after dinner, between two of them, respecting the driving of a wagon up a very difficult hill. Hot words were followed, almost instantly, by blows-one with a knife, or dagger, which proved fatal in about twenty minutes. The man was buried the next morning. Feeling respecting the affair ran high, and the survivor very soon left the company, alone, his family being constrained to remain in it, by the previous loss of their cattle, on the desert."

William Graves described the fateful encounter in even more detail: "We had a rule in traveling which we always observed, and that was, if one wagon drove in the lead one day it should fall in the rear the next, so as to allow everyone his turn in the lead…Snider said that his team could pull up alone; just then Reed had got another team to double to his wagon, and started to pass Snider's oxen. Reed…said to Snider, 'you have no business here in the way,' Snider said 'it is my place'…Reed ran to him and stuck a large six-inch butcher's knife into his heart and cut off two ribs. Snider then turned the butt-end of his whip stock and struck at him three times…Snider…died in five minutes…Some of the company were opposed to allowing Reed to travel in the company; so they agreed to banish him…"

Despite the horrific nature of the incident, Reed's exile was harrowing, as Eliza Donner noted: "Mr. Reed maintained that the deed was not prompted by malice, that he had acted in self-defence and in defence of his wife; and that he would not be driven from his helpless, dependent family. The assembly promised that the company would care for his family, and limited his stay in camp. His wife, fearing the consequence of noncompliance with the sentence, begged him to abide by it, and to push on to the settlement, procure food and assistance, and return for her and their children. The following morning, after participating in the funeral rites over the lamented dead, Mr. Reed took leave of his friends and sorrowing family and left the camp." Later, John Breen would write with the benefit of hindsight, "Reed left the company on horseback and alone leaving his family with the company, I have always thought that this was a misfortune for the whole party as Reed was an intelligent and energetic Man, and if he had remained the party might have got through - He said that he would go before and endeavor to send help back as provisions were now getting scarce."

With one of their ablest leaders gone, the Donner Party continued along the Humboldt River, only to be attacked just a few days later by Paiute raiders. As supplies dwindled and the animals grew weaker, the people resorted to walking instead of riding in the wagons, and things continued to fall apart when the group forced the elderly Mr. Hardkoop to walk as well. Hardkoop walked for as long as he could until his feet could no longer carry him, and as he sat by a stream, he was left behind to die. Meanwhile, Mr. Wolfinger decided to remain behind to cache his wagon, which meant he gathered everything he could carry on horseback and left the rest in hopes of getting back to it in the future. He never caught up with the party and was presumed killed by groups of wandering Native Americans.

Stanton finally made it back to the group in late October, but McCutchen was too ill to return with him and stayed back at the fort to recover. Virginia Reed recalled, "On the 19th of October, while traveling along the Truckee, our hearts were gladdened by the return of Stanton, with seven mules loaded with provisions. Mr. McCutchen was ill and could not travel, but Captain Sutter had sent two of his Indian vaqueros, Luis and Salvador with Stanton. Hungry as we were, Stanton brought us something better than food--news that my father was alive. Stanton had met him nor far from Sutter's Fort; he had been three days without food, and his horse was not able to carry him. Stanton had given him a horse and some provisions and he had gone on. We now packed what little we had left on one mule and started with Stanton. My mother rode on a mule, carrying Tommy in her lap; Patty and Jim rode behind the two Indians, and I behind Mr. Stanton, and in this way we journeyed on through the rain..."

Bruce C. Cooper's 2003 picture of the Truckee River

Unfortunately, the rain soon turned to snow, and now everyone knew that their time was running out. The party lost another man when William Pike died from an accidental gunshot wound, and George Donner severely injured his hand while repairing a broken wagon axle, limiting his usefulness in the camp. Around the same time, Eliza Donner described a scary encounter with a Native American on October 22: "That day we crossed the Truckee River for the forty-ninth and last time in eighty miles, and encamped for the night at the top of a high hill, where we received our last experience of Indian cruelty. The perpetrator was concealed behind a willow, and with savage vim and well trained hand, sent nineteen arrows whizzing through the air, and each arrow struck a different ox. Mr. Eddy caught him in the act; and as he turned to flee, the white man's rifle ball struck him between the shoulders and pierced his body. With a spring into the air and an agonizing shriek, he dropped lifeless into the bushes below. Strange, but true, not an ox was seriously hurt!"

As the days came and went, the group continued to lose cattle as the poor beasts took any chance they could to throw off their ropes and wander away, especially during severe storms. Finally, the decision was reach to go ahead and slaughter the few cattle that were left in order to have enough meat to survive, and some of the men, including William Eddy, hunted when they could. Of course, the wild game were also aware that winter was at hand and had mostly burrowed underground or migrated to warmer regions, so hunters had very little luck.

Concerned about their families, Reed and McCutchen left the safety of the fort with what provisions they could carry and made their way toward the last known location of the party. However, the snow soon drove them back to safety, forcing them to cache their provisions along the way in the hopes of returning in a few days.

Near the end of October, Eliza Donner recalled how they received some of the bad news that portended the party's disastrous future:

> "Much as we felt the shock, there was little time for self-indulgence. Never were moments of greater importance; for while father and uncle were hewing a new axle, two men came from the head of the company to tell about the snow. It was a terrible piece of news!
>
> "Those men reported that on the twenty-eighth of that month the larger part of the train had reached a deserted cabin near Truckee Lake (the sheet of water now known as Donner Lake) at the foot of Frémont's Pass in the main chain of the Sierra Nevada Mountains. The following morning they had proceeded to within three miles of the summit; but finding snow there five feet in depth, the trail obliterated, and no place for making camp, they were obliged to return to the spot they had left early in the day. There, they said, the company had assembled to discuss the next move, and great confusion prevailed as the excited members gave voice to their bitterest fears. Some proposed to abandon the wagons and make the oxen carry out the children and provisions; some wanted to take the children and rations and start out on foot; and some sat brooding in dazed silence through the long night.
>
> "The messengers further stated that on the thirtieth, with Stanton as leader, and despite the falling sleet and snow, the forward section of the party united in another

desperate effort to cross the summit, but encountered deeper drifts and greater difficulties. As darkness crept over the whitened waste, wagons became separated and lodged in the snow; and all had to cling to the mountain-side until break of day, when the train again returned to its twice abandoned camp, having been compelled, however, to leave several of the wagons where they had become stalled. The report concluded with the statement that the men at once began log-cutting for cabins in which the company might have to pass the winter."

   Hoping that the bad weather would soon pass, the Donner Party made camp along Alder Creek, building three small shelters with the materials they had on hand, primarily brush, tents and quilts. Other families built their homes closer to Truckee Lake and the stream that fed from it, and over the next month, many would leave their little shelters to make desperate attempts over the Sierra Nevada mountains. According to Jean Baptiste Trudeau, whom the Donner's had hired on back at Fort Bridger, "The Reeds and Graves people were in the advance party, while the Donners, George and Jacob, and their families, were in the party left behind. Our little band worked bravely on until we came to Alder Creek Valley, where we had to stop, it being impossible to go further. The snow came on with blinding fury and being unable to build cabins we put up brush sheds, covering them with limbs from the pine trees. It was the first of November, I think, that we went into that camp of snow and suffering..." Even those who wanted to leave had trouble doing so, as related by Eliza Donner: "Different parties, both with and without children, had repeatedly endeavored to force their way out of that wilderness of snow, but each in turn had become confused, and unconsciously moved in a circle back to camp. Several persons had become snow-blind. Every landmark was lost, even to Stanton, who had twice crossed the range."

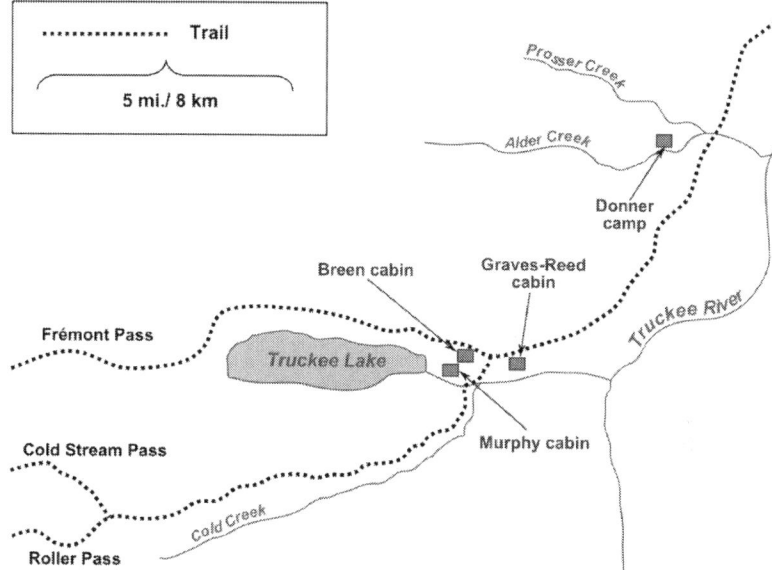

Map of the Donner Party's locations during the winter

The Truckee Lake is now known as Donner Lake, and this picture looks toward the mountain pass used by the Donner Party.

The area where the Donner Party camped during the winter

Trudeau

Chapter 6: The Forlorn Hope

"We had a very slavish day's travel, climbing to the divide. Nothing of interest occurred until reaching the summit. The scenery was too grand for me to pass without notice, the changes being so great; walking now on the loose snow, and now stepping on a hard, slick rock a number of hundred yards in length. Being a little in the rear of the party, I had a chance to observe the company ahead, trudging along with packs on their backs...My shoes were ox-bows, split in two, and rawhide strings woven in, something in form of the old-fashioned, split-bottom chairs...Well do I remember a remark of one of the company made here, that we were about as near heaven as we could get." - Mary Graves

Mary Graves

"Father's face was very grave. His morning caress had all its wonted tenderness, but the merry twinkle was gone from his eye, and the gladsome note from his voice. For eight consecutive days, the fatal snow fell with but few short intermissions. Eight days, in which there was nothing to break the monotony of torturing, inactive endurance, except the necessity of gathering wood, keeping the fires, and cutting anew the steps which led upward, as the snow increased in depth. Hope well-nigh died within us." – Eliza Donner

Under normal circumstances, there might have been regiments of soldiers available to look for and rescue the stranded settlers, but the Mexican-American War had broken out just weeks after the Donner Party left Indianapolis and had drawn most of the solders south to fight. Making matters worse, Reed and McCutchen did not realize how many cattle had been lost and thought that there was still enough food.

Of course, they did not, and the members of the party were becoming too weak to continue trying to scale the mountains, especially since they were now on foot and without guides. William Eddy later wrote of one of their late November efforts: "Not discouraged, and impelled by the increasing scarcity of provisions at the cabins, on the twentieth they tried it again, and succeeded in crossing the divide; but found it was impossible for them to proceed for the want of a pilot, Mr. Stanton having refused to allow the Indians to accompany them on account of not being able to bring the mules out with them, which Mr. Stanton had taken there with provisions from J. A. Sutter's, previous to the falling of the snow. Here again were their warmest hopes blighted; and they again turned with heavy hearts towards their miserable cabins."

On December 6, Charles Stanton announced that when he was a boy in Vermont, his father had taught him how to make snowshoes, and he believed that he could fashion enough pairs for anyone who was able to walk over the mountains. They would then go for help while leaving the weaker members behind with the remainder of the food. On December 15, the party lost its first member to starvation when Baylis Williams died, and those who chose to try to cross with snowshoes, later given the romantic name "Forlorn Hope," left the next morning. 17 of them set out, but William Murphy and Dutch Burger were forced to turn back after the first day, and Charles Stanton would succumb to snow blindness and drop out of the party, destined to die on the side of the trail.

On Christmas Day, the Snowshoe Party was caught on an open mountainside during a blizzard, and according to Mary Graves, "They went on all day without a morsel of food, the rain pouring continuously. At night it ceased. Some were confused in their perceptions, some delirious, some raving. Those who were strong enough to realize their condition, might well now despair. The women bore up better than the men. One of them had a cape or mantle stuffed with raw cotton, and upon a minute examination of it, she found, between the shoulders, about an inch square of the inner surface dry. The lining was cut, and enough taken out to catch the spark from the flint. They lost or left their axe, but were able to make a fire, after much difficulty, of a few gathered boughs. They sat down around it. There was nothing else to be done."

What happened next is a tale so shocking that only those who were there could ever understand it. Patrick Dolan was the first to speak of the unspeakable: that someone should give up his or her life to save the others. If he hoped that his proposal would shock his comrades into some sort of reactive energy to carry on, he was disappointed, because they were now all so overcome with hunger that they agreed with him. The only question in their minds was how to choose the victim. Perhaps subconsciously hoping to keep the inevitable at bay, they carried on a lengthy discussion on the merits of a duel as opposed to some sort of lottery.

In the end, they didn't need to select their first victim, because a young man known to history only by his first name, Antonio, died before the party could decide who to kill, and he was soon joined by Franklin Graves. Decades later, Mary Graves would describe his death in a discreet manner that allowed her to distance herself from the gruesome reality of what was coming: "The father, whose two daughters were of the company, was the first released. The chilling rain had pierced his emaciated frame, and subdued the energy which has resisted courageously all that had gone before...In that desolate hour of death, he called his youngest daughter to his side, and bade her cherish and husband every chance of life, in the fearful days which he knew awaited them... She must revolt at nothing that would keep life in her till she could reach some help for those whom they both loved. He clearly foreshadowed the terrible necessity to which, within a few hours, he saw they must come, and died, leaving his injunction upon her, to yield to it as resolutely as she had done everything else that had been required of her, since their sufferings began."

Ironically, Patrick Dolan, the one who had suggested picking a sacrificial victim for the benefit of the rest of the Forlorn Hope, soon became so weakened from hunger that he was unable to control his body temperature. Dolan deliriously stripped off his clothes and ran naked into the woods. The others were too weak to go after him, but he returned to his senses just long enough to make his way back to the camp, where he died just a few hours later. There were now several dead bodies, and everyone was terribly hungry, but nobody could quite yet resort to what most considered an unspeakable sin.

Chapter 7: "The Terrible Necessity"

"Thursday [December] 31th last of the year. May we with God's help spend the coming year better than the past which we purpose to do if Almighty God will deliver us from our present dreadful situation which is our prayer if the will of God sees it fitting for us. Amen. Morning fair now Cloudy wind E by S. For three days past freezing hard every night looks like another snow storm, snow storms are dreadful to us, snow very deep. Crust on the snow"

It is possible that every member of the Forlorn Hope would have died had it not been for their sense of obligation to a 12 year old boy named Lemuel Murphy. He was obviously dying, and it seems that the hope of saving him is what drove the others to make their first grisly cut into Patrick Dolan's body. Taking a portion of the cold, bloody flesh, Lemuel's sister tried to get him to eat, but he was now too weak to even chew and died.

The two Native Americans with the group, Salvador and Luis, refused to partake of human flesh, perhaps because it was too far removed from their sense of decency or because they were more accustomed to going without food. At first, William Eddy also refused to cannibalize but did not try to stop the others; a few days later, he began to join them in their sustenance.

As members of the Forlorn Hope resigned themselves to cannibalism, those who had eaten began to feel stronger, and they began butchering the human carcasses much like they were accustomed to doing with a cow or pig and preserving the flesh and organs for future use. Still retaining some sensitivity, the group divided the meat in such a way as to make sure no one would have to eat the remains of one of their relatives, and with everything packed, they left their camp and continued hiking along the trail. However, once they were moving again, their hunger inevitably increased, and they soon consumed all the flesh they had brought with them. Fearing hunger even more now that they had experienced it, some of the group began to chew on the ox hide straps of their snowshoes.

Yet again, the discussion arose as to who might die so that the others could live, but this time it took on an even more sinister tone. Perhaps feeling judged by the only two among them who had the fortitude not to cannibalize, the group began considering killing their native guides, Luis and Salvador. Though willing to commit cannibalism, William Eddy still drew the line at murder, so he warned the two men to leave the camp when no one was looking, but Jay Fosdick died that night anyway. Still hoping that he might get something better to eat than a corpse, Eddy took Mary Graves, the healthiest member of the group, and went hunting with her. They returned to the camp with a small deer only to learn their cohorts had begun to cannibalize Fosdick's body in their absence. Eddy later gave the most detailed account of what happened to Fosdick's body: "Mrs. Fosdick had been with her husband during the previous night, which was bitterly cold; and after his death, she rolled his body in the only blanket they possessed, and laid herself down upon the ground, desiring to die, and hoping that she would freeze to death...But the return of the morning's light brought with it an instinctive love of life, and she now proposed to go back to the body of her husband... Two individuals accompanied her, and notwithstanding the remonstrances, entreaties, and tears of the affected widow, cut out the heart and liver, and severed the arms and legs of her departed husband."

When they were once again strengthened by the deer and other less palatable meat, the seven remaining survivors set off again, only to come across Luis and Salvador along the trail. With nothing to eat, the group watched as William Foster pulled out his gun and shot the two dead. They would be the last humans eaten by the Forlorn Hope.

Meanwhile, back at the camp on Alder Creek, starvation began to pick off its victims one at a time. By December 21, Jacob Donner James Smith, Samuel Shoemaker and Joseph Reinhardt were dead, and Dutch Burger died on December 29. But even in the midst of such tragedy, the coming holiday was not lost, and decades later, Virginia Reed wrote, "Christmas was near, but to the starving its memory gave no comfort. It came and passed without observance, but my mother had determined weeks before that her children should have a treat on this one day. She had laid away a few dried apples, some beans, a bit of tripe, and a small piece of bacon. When this hoarded store was brought out, the delight of the little ones knew no bounds. The cooking was watched carefully, and when we sat down to our Christmas dinner mother said, 'Children, eat slowly for this one day you can have all you wish.' So bitter was the misery relieved by that one bright day, that I have never since sat down to a Christmas dinner without my thoughts going back to Donner Lake."

Chapter 8: Survival

"EMIGRANTS IN THE MOUNTAINS. It is probably not generally known to the people, that there is now in the California mountains in a most distressing situation a party of emigrants from the United States, who were prevented from crossing the mountains by an early heavy fall of snow. The party consists of about sixty persons, men, women and children. They were, almost entirely out of provisions, when they reached the foot of the mountain, and but for the timely succor afforded them by Capt. J.A. Sutter, one of the most humane and liberal men in California, they must have all perished in a few days. Captain Sutter as soon as he ascertained their situation, sent five mules loaded with provisions to them. A second party was dispatched with provisions for them, but they found the mountain impassable, in consequence of the snow. We hope that our citizens will do something for the relief of these unfortunate people." - *The California Star*, January 16, 1847

An 1866 picture of trees that had been cut by the Donner Party near Alder Creek

On January 12, 1847 the seven remaining members of the Forlorn Hope finally came in contact with other people when a group of Native Americans, unaware of what had transpired, welcomed them and shared with the starving party their meager stores of acorns. They then led them to the nearest white settlement, the Johnson Ranch. As soon as they arrived, the Forlorn Hope began telling their sad story and begging for help to rescue their loved ones back at the camp. George Tucker, who worked on the ranch, later recalled, "As Soon as we got these Seven in and got them made as Comfortable as Circumstances would admit and learned the Condition of the rest of the Company they had left behind we then Commenced to devise Some plan to relieve them. But at Johnson's Ranch there was only 3 or 4 families of poor Emigrants beside Johnsons and nothing could be done without help from other Settlements…John Rhodes, one of our neighbors, an Emigrant that had crossed the plains that Season Said if there was no other way he would go on foot. We had no means of crossing the river so we made a boat by lashing 2 pine logs together with Strips of rawhide."

While his family and friends were starving, James Reed had moved on with his life, oblivious to what was going on. After fighting for a few months in the Mexican-American War, he finally made it to California and filed a claim for land for he and each adult member of his family. On January 18, he spent the day planting fruit trees on the land in order to shore up his claim to it, while on that very same day, his daughter Virginia reported, "We had nothing to eat but ox hides…Eliza had to go to Mr. Graves' cabin & we stayed at Mr. Breen…We had to kill little Cash the dog & eat him. We ate his head and feet & hide & everything about him" Later, she would report, "We now had nothing to eat but raw hides and they were on the roof of the cabin to keep out the snow; when prepared for cooking and boiled they were simply a pot of glue."

Meanwhile, Patrick Breen was still keeping his diary, writing on January 24, "Some cloudy this morning. Ceased snowing yesterday about 2 o'clock. Wind about S.E. All in good health thanks be to God for his Mercies endureth forever. Heard nothing from Murphy's camp since the storm. Expect to hear they suffered some." Two days later, he added, "Cleared up yesterday. Today fine & pleasant, wind S. In hopes we are done with snow storms, those that went to [Sutter's Fort[not yet returned. Provisions getting very scant. People getting weak living on short allowance of hides"

Thursd. 25th froze hard last night fine & sunshiny to day wind W. Mrs Murphy says the wolves are about to dig up the dead bodies at her shanty the nights are too cold to watch them, we hear them howl.

Frid 26th froze hard last night to day clear & warm Wind S:E: blowing briskly Marthas jaw swelled with the toothache hungry times in camp, plenty hides but the folks will not eat them we eat them with a tolerable good apetite. Thanks be to Almighty God. Amen

Mrs Murphy said here yesterday that thought she would commence on Milt. & eat him. I dont that she has done so yet, it is distressing The Donnos told the California folks that they commence to eat the dead people 4 days ago, if they did not succeed that day or next in finding their cattle then under ten or twelve feet of snow & did not know the spot or near it, I suppose they have done ere this time.

A page from Breen's diary

As the Forlorn Hope was beginning to recover at the ranch, those camped along the river were dying at an increasing rate. The Keseberg family, which had forced old Mr. Hardkoop to walk and all but consigned him to death, lost their infant son on January 24. A week later, on the same day that the First Relief team left Sutter's Fort, Landrum Murphy died. Years later, his brother would describe his death: "Then my eldest brother was very weak, and almost at death's door, and my mother went to the [Breens], and begged a small piece of meat; just a few mouthfuls. This is in the history recorded by Mr. [Breen}. I remember the little piece of meat; my mother gave half of it to my dying brother, and he ate it, fell off to sleep, with hollow death-gurgling snore, and when the sound ceased, I went to him, and he was dead - starved to death in my presence. My mother said that if she had known he was going to die, she would have given him the balance of the meat while she was starving too; and she had her two little boys, her daughter, three little children all of us starving, waiting for relief."

Landrum Murphy was followed in early February by Harriet McCutchen, Margaret and Eleanor Eddy, Augustus Spitzer, and Milt Elliot. On February 18, the First Relief reached the camp with food and other necessities, and the next day, the team made its way to the nearby Alder Creek camp where the Donner's were. Rounding up the 23 people who were strong enough to travel, the First Relief began escorting them back to the ranch on January 21. Two of the Reed children, Patty and Tommy, were not up for the journey and returned to stay with the Breen's, while Ada Keseberg and John Denton both died along the trail back. Tragically, young William Hook also died, but not from starvation; his delicate system could not take the sudden return of full meals, so he died from overeating.

Chapter 9: Rescue

An 1868 picture of Donner Lake from the mountain pass

"Finally we concluded we would go or die trying, for not to make any attempt to save them would be a disgrace to us and to California for as long as time lasted. We started, a small company of 7 men, myself, John Rhoads, Joseph Forster, Mr. Glover and some sailors. We each carried 50 pounds of provisions, a heavy blanket, tools and started...After we reached the mountains the snow was 5 to 25 feet deep. We made snow shoes out of pine boughs. At the end of our day's travel we cached some provisions to have on our way back...We were seven days going to them. The people were dying every day. They had been living on dead bodies for weeks." - Daniel Rhoads

Even though the First Relief had arrived and rescued some, many who stayed behind were still aware of the dangers they faced. Georgia Donner remembered how her parents prepared human flesh for them, "Father was crying and did not look at us the entire time, and we little ones felt we could not help it. There was nothing else." Eliza Donner recalled:

"As father grew weaker, we children spent more time upon the snow above camp.

Often, after his wound was dressed and he fell into a quiet slumber, our ever-busy, thoughtful mother would come to us and sit on the tree trunk. Sometimes she brought paper and wrote; sometimes she sketched the mountains and the tall tree-tops, which now looked like small trees growing up through the snow. And often, while knitting or sewing, she held us spell-bound with wondrous tales of 'Joseph in Egypt,' of 'Daniel in the den of lions,' of 'Elijah healing the widow's son,' of dear little Samuel, who said, 'Speak Lord, for Thy servant heareth,' and of the tender, loving Master, who took young children in his arms and blessed them.

"With me sitting on her lap, and Frances and Georgia at either side, she referred to father's illness and lonely condition, and said that when the next 'Relief' came, we little ones might be taken to the settlement, without either parent, but, God willing, both would follow later. Who could be braver or tenderer than she, as she prepared us to go forth with strangers and live without her? While she, without medicine, without lights, would remain and care for our suffering father, in hunger and in cold, and without her little girls to kiss good-morning and good-night. She taught us how to gain friends among those whom we should meet, and what to answer when asked whose children we were…

"The last food which I remember seeing in our camp before the arrival of the Second Relief was a thin mould of tallow, which mother had tried out of the trimmings of the jerked beef brought us by the First Relief. She had let it harden in a pan, and after all other rations had given out, she cut daily from it three small white squares for each of us, and we nibbled off the four corners very slowly, and then around and around the edges of the precious pieces until they became too small for us to hold between our fingers."

By this time, James Reed had gotten word about what was happening, so he began to round up men and supplies to launch his own rescue mission, but by the time he arrived on March 1, those left behind had succumbed to starvation and madness and had also begun to eat their dead neighbors. After taking only a small amount of time to give them some of the food he had brought with him, Reed left the lake area with the Breen's and the many children who had been left in their charge, as well as Elizabeth Graves and her children.

The problem at this point was that no one knew how long it would be until another search party arrived, and the first two parties had no idea how desperate the circumstances were for the people they were rescuing. As a result, neither of the first two groups brought along enough provisions to help the starving people hold out for much longer. According to Elizabeth Keseberg, "When Reed's relief party left the cabins, Mr. Reed left me a half teacupful of flour, and about half a pound of jerked beef. It was all he could give. Mrs. Murphy, who was left with me, because too weak and emaciated to walk, had no larger portion. Reed had no animosity toward me. He found me too weak to move. He washed me, combed my hair, and treated me kindly. Indeed, he had no cause to do otherwise. Some of my portion of the flour brought by Stanton from Sutter's Fort I gave to Reed's children, and thus saved their lives. When he left me, he promised to return in two weeks and carry me over the mountains. When this party left, I was not able to stand, much less to walk."

On March 5, the Second Relief party became trapped itself in Summit Valley and were forced to take shelter in the infamous "Starved Camp" where the Forlorn Hope had camped. While they were there, 5 year old Isaac Donner died, and it became clear that most of the other children were in no shape to continue their journey. Carrying Patty and Tommy on their backs, Reed and Hiram Miller (who had accompanied him on the rescue mission) continued on their way, joined only by Solomon Hook, who was old enough and strong enough to walk. Their plan was to look for food and supplies that they had cached along the way and hopefully return with it to help the others.

On March 13, the Third Relief, headed by William Foster and William Eddy, arrived at the Starved Camp, where they discovered that those left behind had resorted to cannibalizing Isaac Donner and two others who had died during the wait for help. Leaving John Stark to watch that group, Eddy and Foster trekked forward to the lake camp in hopes of finding their sons and others, but by the time they arrived, both little boys were dead. Elizabeth Donner and her son Lewis were also dead, and George Donner was dying as a result of his wound, which now had gangrene. Tamsen, his wife, refused to leave him but sent her children with the party. Trudeau and Nicholas Clark initially offered to stay behind and care for George and Tamsen Donner, as well and several others who were too weak to travel, but they soon changed their minds and rushed out to catch up with the Third Relief.

After the Third Relief, bad weather set in again and prevented anyone from making it back to the camps until mid-March. By then, Louis Keseberg was the only person left at the camp who was still alive, and he survived by subsisting off the dead bodies of his friends to survive. He later reported, "Oh! the days and weeks of horror which I passed in that camp! I had no hope of being rescued, until I saw the green grass coming up by the spring on the hillside, and the wild geese coming to nibble it. The birds were coming back to their breeding grounds, and I felt that I could kill them for food. I also had plenty of tobacco and a good meerschaum pipe, and almost the only solace I enjoyed was smoking. In my weak condition it took me two or three hours every day to get sufficient wood to keep my fire going."

At first, it must have seemed to Keseberg that the worst of his experiences were over once the Fourth Relief showed up to escort him west, but he soon suffered an even worse shock. He later explained, "One day I was dragging myself slowly along behind the party, when I came to a place which had evidently been used as a camping ground by some of the previous parties. Feeling very tired, I thought it would be a good place to make some coffee. Kindling a fire, I filled my coffee-pot with fresh snow and sat waiting for it to melt and get hot. Happening to case my eyes carelessly around, I discovered a little piece of calico protruding from the snow.

Half thoughtlessly, half out of idle curiosity, I caught hold of the cloth, and finding it did not come readily, I gave it a strong pull. I had in my hands the body of my dead child Ada! She had been buried in the snow which, melting down, had disclosed a portion of her clothing. I thought I should go frantic! It was the first intimation I had of her death, and it came with such a shock!"

Keseberg arrived with the Fourth Relief at Sutter's Fort on April 29, 1847, but not before members of that relief expedition were haunted by their own findings. One of them, William Fallon, wrote, "April 17th. Reached the Cabins between 12 and 1 o'clock. Expected to find some of the sufferers alive, Mrs. Donner and Kiesburg in particular. Entered the cabins and a horrible scene presented itself,--human bodies terribly mutilated, legs, arms, and sculls scattered in every direction. One body, supposed to be that of Mrs. Eddy, lay near the entrance, the limbs severed off and a frightful gash in the skull. The flesh from the bones was nearly consumed and a painful stillness pervaded the place. The supposition was that all were dead, when a sudden shout revived our hopes, and we flew in the direction of the sound, three Indians were hitherto concealed, started from the ground and fled at our approach, leaving behind their bows and arrows. We delayed two hours in searching the cabins, during which we were obliged to witness sights from which we would have…turned away, and which are too dreadful to put on record." -

Chapter 10: Life From Death

"We had bread and milk for supper that night, and the same good food next day. In the afternoon we were taken across the river in an Indian canoe. Then we followed the winding path through the tules to Sutter's Fort, where we were given over to our half-sisters by those heroic men who had kept their pledge to our mother and saved our lives." – Eliza Donner

Naturally, the surviving members of the Donner Party who went through the harrowing experience were not inclined to talk about it, but as the years passed and rumors spread, one member of the doomed Donner Party after another came forward to tell their version of the desperate struggle for survival. Even still, few would ever have imagined what General Stephen W. Kearny and his company found when they arrived on June 22 at what would later be called the "Cannibal Camp." One of his men later wrote, "A more revolting or appalling spectacle I never witnessed. The remains here, by order of Gen. Kearny collected and buried under the superintendence of Major Swords. They were interred in a pit which had been dug in the center of one of the cabins for a cache. These melancholy duties to the dead being performed, the cabins, by order of Major Swords, were fired, and with everything surrounded them connected with this horrid and melancholy tragedy, were consumed." Despite that description, one body did survive unscathed: "The body of George Donner was found at his camp, about eight or ten miles distant, wrapped in a sheet. He was buried by a party of men detailed for that purpose."

Kearny

The numbers can never tell the entire story of any historical event, but they can provide a sense of the magnitude of what happened. Little more than half of the 87 people who chose to leave the main wagon train and join the Donner Party survived their trip, and most of them were children who survived either because they needed less food to survive or because their parents starved themselves to save them. Others were sent off with the relief groups while the parents stayed behind, often to die. The children of both Jacob and George Donner lost both their parents, as did those of Franklin Graves. On the other hand, William Eddy lost his entire family, and the Murphy parents lost most of their children.

Those who did survive were mostly destitute as a result of losing all their livestock and nearly all their possessions, and while that paled in comparison to the deaths of dozens of people, the loss of property and the psychological scars ensured the survivors suffered mightily. While the widowers struggled to find new ways to support their families, several widows quickly remarried. The Reed family settled in San Jose and raised two of Jacob Donner's children with their own, while the other Donner children were adopted by a couple living near Sutter's Fort.

Georgia and Eliza Donner with Mrs. Brunner circa 1850

The four younger surviving children of the Graves family were primarily raised by their three older siblings. Sarah Graves, who was left a young widow, and Mary Graves both married within a year of their rescue. Along with their brother William, they took their younger siblings into their homes. 9 year old Nancy would remain the one most scarred by her ordeal, but none of the children were unscathed. While many would go on to tell their stories in both public and private settings, Nancy refused to talk to anyone or to give any sort of written account of what she went through. Many assumed that she never got over a sense of guilt for surviving off the remains of dead relatives.

William Eddy and Louis Keseberg were also haunted by their actions and decisions for the rest of their lives, and in fact, many believed that Keseberg had actually murdered Tamsen Donner, although he never stood trial for the crime. Rescuers grew suspicious when they found Keseberg had a pot of human flesh and several possessions owned by George Donner, including gold. William Eddy was among his accusers and even plotted to kill Keseberg himself before deciding such a deed would do more harm than good. After all, enough people had died.

The Breen's and the Reed's continued to fare better than their traveling companions. Mary Reed was anxious to make sure no one else made the mistakes her family had; in a letter back home to family after her rescue, she wrote, "I will now give you some good and friendly advice. Stay at home,—you are in a good place, where, if sick, you are not in danger of starving to death." Isabella Breen, who was a year old during that dreadful winter, was the last surviving member of the party, dying in 1935.

The State of California has referred to the Donner Party's story as "an isolated and tragic incident of American history that has been transformed into a major folk epic," but perhaps the best perspective on the entire event came from the pen of Virginia Reed, who concluded a long letter to her cousin with these words of wisdom: "I have not wrote to you half the trouble we have had but I have wrote enough to let you know that you don't know what trouble is. But thank God we have all got through and the only family that did not eat human flesh. We have left everything but I don't care for that. We have got through with our lives but don't let this letter dishearten anybody. Never take no cutoffs and hurry along as fast as you can."

This monument commemorates the Donner Party in Donner Park, and the statue intentionally sits on a 22 foot pedestal to mark how high the drifts were that trapped them.

Bibliography

Dixon, Kelly (ed) (2011). *An Archaeology of Desperation: Exploring the Donner Party's Alder Creek Camp*, University of Oklahoma Press.

Hardesty, Donald (1997). *The Archaeology of the Donner Party*, University of Nevada Press.

Johnson, Kristin (ed.)(1996). *Unfortunate Emigrants: Narratives of the Donner Party*, Utah State University Press.

King, Joseph (1992). *Winter of Entrapment: A New Look at the Donner Party*, P. D. Meany Company.

McGlashan, Charles (1879). *History of the Donner Party: A Tragedy of the Sierra Nevada*: 11th edition (1918), A Carlisle & Company, San Francisco.

McNeese, Tim (2009). *The Donner Party: A Doomed Journey*, Chelsea House Publications.

Rarick, Ethan (2008). *Desperate Passage: The Donner Party's Perilous Journey West*, Oxford University Press.

Stewart, George R. (1936). *Ordeal by Hunger: The Story of the Donner Party*: supplemented edition (1988), Houghton Mifflin.

Made in the USA
Monee, IL
01 October 2021